First Facts ™

Learning about Money

Earning Money

by Mary Firestone

Consultant:
Sharon M. Danes, PhD
Professor and Family Economist
University of Minnesota

Capstone press
Mankato, Minnesota

First Facts is published by Capstone Press
151 Good Counsel Drive, P.O. Box 669, Mankato, Minnesota 56002
www.capstonepress.com

Library of Congress Cataloging-in-Publication Data
Firestone, Mary.
    Earning money / by Mary Firestone.
    p. cm.—(First facts. Learning about money)
    Includes bibliographical references and index.
    ISBN 0-7368-2639-4 (hardcover)
    1. Money-making projects for children—Juvenile literature. 2. Money—Juvenile literature.
3. Work—Juvenile literature. I. Title.
HF5392.F57 2005
650.1'2—dc22   2004000392

Summary: Simple text and photographs discuss how and why people earn money.

Editorial Credits

Heather Adamson, editor; Jennifer Bergstrom, designer; Enoch Peterson, illustrator;
    Scott Thoms, photo researcher; Eric Kudalis, product planning editor

Photo Credits

Brand X Pictures, cover
Capstone Press/Gary Sundermeyer, 5 (foreground), 9, 11, 12–13, 14 (foreground), 15, 16–17
    (foreground), 19
Comstock Inc., back cover, 1
Corbis, 5 (background) 14 (background); Owen Franken, 6–7; Richard Hamilton Smith, 10;
    Ted Spiegel, 8
Photodisc, 16–17 (background)
The Chocolate Farm/Neal Stafford, 20

1 2 3 4 5 6 09 08 07 06 05 04

Table of Contents

Earning Money

Sam pours lemonade into a cup and takes a quarter from the customer. He has **earned** $3 selling drinks today. Sam **wants** to buy a model car. People earn money to buy the things they **need** and want.

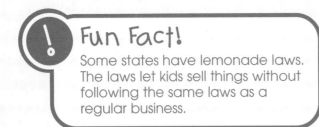

Fun Fact!
Some states have lemonade laws. The laws let kids sell things without following the same laws as a regular business.

Working

People earn money by working. They trade their time and **skills** for money. Sam's mom works as a cook. She gets paid to make food.

Kids can work too. They can trade their time and skills for money.

Fun Fact!
In 2000, about 2 million people in the United States earned money cooking.

7

Selling Services

People earn money by selling services. Window washers sell window cleaning services. Schools pay teachers for their teaching services.

Kids can earn money selling
services. Sam walks dogs and shovels
snow for neighbors.

Selling Goods

People earn money selling **goods**. Farmers sell crops they grow. Artists sell artwork they make. Grocers sell items they buy from other food makers.

Kids can earn money selling goods. Sam gathers his old toys to sell. He sells his goods to friends and neighbors.

Fair Prices

Earning money depends on fair **prices**. Old toys are worth less than new toys. The price of an old toy should be less than a new one.

Fair prices include costs. Lemons and cups cost money. A fair price for lemonade is a little more than the costs of supplies.

Lemonade 25¢

Changing Prices

Prices change based on how much people want to buy something. On hot days, Sam charges more for his drinks. People are thirstier on hot days.

People look for low prices. When several kids want to shovel snow, Sam charges less for the same work. People often **hire** the worker who charges less.

Earning Allowances

Some parents pay their children **allowances**. Kids earn allowances for being part of the family or for doing **chores**.

Sam earns extra money at home by doing more chores. He paints a bench for his dad.

Fun Fact!
In 1910, about 2 million American children worked in factories to help support their families.

Earning Your Own Money

It feels good to work for money. When you earn money, you do not need other people to buy things for you. Sam used the money he earned to buy a model car.

Amazing but True!

Elise Macmillan started selling homemade chocolates when she was 9 years old. In 1999, she started a business called the Chocolate Farm. It sells chocolates in the shape of farm animals. The business has earned millions of dollars.

Hands On: Have a Sale

You can earn money by having a sale. Ask your parents if you can sell things you no longer need or want. Invite friends and neighbors to your sale.

What You Need

old toys, clothes, or items you can sell
table
pen
tape
markers and posterboard
notebook
shoebox and extra money for making change

What You Do

1. Gather old toys, clothes, or items you can sell. Set them out on the table. Put similar items near each other.
2. Decide on a fair price for each item. Write the price on a piece of tape and stick it to the item.
3. Use markers and posterboard to make signs about your sale. Tape the signs around the neighborhood.
4. Keep a record of each item you sell in a notebook. Put the money you collect in a shoebox. When the sale is over, you can put your money in a bank. Take down the signs when the sale is finished.

Glossary

allowance (uh-LOU-uhnss)—money given to someone regularly

chore (CHOR)—a daily or weekly task or job

earn (URN)—to receive payment for working

goods (GUDZ)—things that can be bought or sold

hire (HIRE)—to agree to pay someone to do work for you

need (NEED)—to require something; you need food, shelter, and clothes to stay alive.

price (PRISSE)—the amount that must be paid for something

skill (SKIL)—the ability to do something well

want (WONT)—to feel you would like to have something; you may want a new bike or a snack.

Read More

Thayer, Tanya. *Earning Money*. First Step Nonfiction. Minneapolis: Lerner, 2002.

Tillema, Juliana O. *The Young Zillionaire's Guide to Producing Goods and Services.* Be a Zillionaire. New York: Rosen, 2000.

Internet Sites

FactHound offers a safe, fun way to find Internet sites related to this book. All of the sites on FactHound have been researched by our staff.

Here's how:
1. Visit *www.facthound.com*
2. Type in this special code **0736826394** for age-appropriate sites. Or enter a search word related to this book for a more general search.
3. Click on the **Fetch It** button.

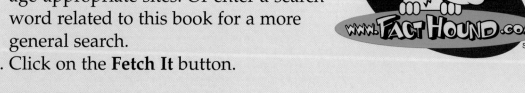

FactHound will fetch the best sites for you!

Index